THE ROAD TO EPHESUS

A 1952 Odyssey through the Balkans and Turkey

– Report by an Irish student hitch-hiker –

JOHN S. JOYCE

BCS

PUBLISHED BY   B C S

First printing, November 2017

ISBN 978-1-9998410-0-3

.

Foreword

Dublin-born John Joyce lived the first 18 years of his life in the family home "Woodview", off Mount Merrion Avenue in Blackrock, County Dublin. After graduating in engineering at University College Dublin in 1954, he joined Siemens in Germany. He worked as an engineer for that company until his retirement after 42 years, a career which involved, much to his liking, extensive travelling throughout all five continents, including a 13-year assignment in the USA. Now he lives in a faithfully renovated 14th century house in the heart of Bamberg's old city, very close to the cathedral.

His adventurous spirit became evident before he left Ireland's shores, however. Having in 1951 travelled around North Africa, in the summer of 1952 he undertook an even more unusual adventure. It took more than a little courage for a solitary young Irishman to set off in the summer of 1952 into the then Communist Yugoslavia, as well as Turkey and Greece, with little in the way of funds and virtually no contacts to help him on his way. This is what John Joyce did, and did with a minimum of fuss and fear.

John, who is extremely modest, both now and in his Irish Times reports, about his exploits, augmented his meagre funds while on the journey by writing articles for Yugoslav, Greek and Turkish newspapers about Ireland – just as his near namesake (but no relation) James Joyce did in Trieste in the early years of the last century. Accentuating the James Joyce connection, John Joyce's twenty thousand kilometers odyssey began in Trieste, where he was hosted for a couple of nights by the writer's brother Stanislaus, who had lived there since 1905, before he set out on the first leg of his journey, into Yugoslavia. He made his way by hitching lifts, relying on the generosity of the people he met – and he was rarely let down.

It is fascinating to read his account of life in the state dominated by the figure of Josep Broz Tito: in many ways it was a typical Communist state – authoritarian, controlling, enforcing a deadening uniformity – but there were also some differences, since Tito had already broken with the Soviet Union, and people spoke more freely to John than they might have done otherwise. Now that this phase of Yugoslavia's history is over – and the country itself no longer exists – John's testimony to his experience there, the experience of a highly intelligent, observant Westerner, is particularly valuable. From Yugoslavia, John made his way to Greece, where, after the dullness and greyness of Communist Yugoslavia, he was very struck by the colour and the brightness of the scene. As in Yugoslavia, he was very much a rara avis in those parts, exciting great curiosity among the locals – another sharp reminder of how different the world was then. He next made his way to the islands of the Cyclades group, where he has many acute observations on the incredible archaeological remains that the is-lands contain, and also on how much the remains dominate the life of the country – as he calls it, "land of the living dead".

A highlight of his voyage, in more ways than one, was his visit to Mount Athos, the legendary Greek Orthodox monastery complex that lies atop the "holy mountain" in northeastern Greece (it is in fact an autonomous state within Greece). Visiting Mount Athos was actually the original purpose of John's journey: he had two big advantages in getting there – first, he was a man (essential) and secondly he had a letter of introduction from the Patriarch of Constantinople, to whom he had written much more in hope than expectation. He describes very vividly the life of the complex, and conveys the sense of a world entirely isolated from everything around it, nestling high up on its mountain, indifferent to the passing centuries. Among other feats, he met an ancient Russian Orthodox hermit, who discoursed knowledgeably about Saint Kevin.

From Greece, he continued on to Turkey, visiting the ancient "cone country" of Cappadocia, and eventually made his way to Ephesus, his last destination, where, like everyone who goes there, he was amazed at the completeness of the Roman remains, and explored the remarkable sights – including the alleged last resid-ence of the Virgin Mary – that lie around it.

On Turkey and the Turks, also, he has many very sharp observations. It's no surprise that The Irish Times, in 1952, jumped at the chance to run this fascinating series of articles, bringing a unique Irish perspective to an at that time little-known world. In addition to the fine content, John also took many photographs, seven of which were used to illustrate the series. These have been notably enhanced by his friend Brian Coleman's computerised transcription. The resurrection of these pieces in a reprintable edition is not just a labour of love, it is a fitting tribute to an adventurous Irishman, who blazed a trail for many of his compat-riots to follow.

Terence Killeen

Research Scholar, James Joyce Centre, Dublin
Former journalist, Irish Times

I dedicate this reprint of my ten 1953 newspaper articles post-humously to my father who encouraged me in all my adventurous pursuits.

ACKNOWLEDGEMENTS

I am deeply grateful to my friend *Brian Coleman* who on reading my youthful report, immediately volunteered to reproduce it by means of his computer system which he did with great diligence so as to make it available as an authentic 65-year old documentation to interested people outside my family.

Mr. W. J. (Jack) White, the Features Editor of the *Irish Times*, edited my ten instalments, thereby selecting appropriate headings and inserting subtitles into my text. He also wrote the brief intro-duction which appeared below the published map.

Finally, I also express my gratitude to the *Irish Times* for kind permission to reproduce these articles in book form.

J.S.J.

Contents

Introduction

Presumably in Spring 1952, I had at the age of 20 years and busy studying mechanical and electrical engineering at University College Dublin, stumbled on a brief newspaper report on Mount Athos, of which I had never previously heard. I was so fascinated by the account of this monks' theocratic autonomous republic, that I decided to try and visit it in the course of my planned hitch-hiking 'Grand Tour' to Turkey the following Summer. In 1951, I had hitch-hiked to Morocco and Mauritania; traversing France, Spain and Portugal. Due to illness and running out of time, I did not make it to Timbuktu, but just to the not far distant Tindouf, an important oasis where large numbers of nomadic Tuareg 'blue men' used to frequent. (I wrote two articles on Morocco which appeared in *The Irish Press* newspaper.)

I hit upon the idea of writing to the Ecumenical Patriarch of Constantinople in Istanbul. Since I had no address, I was uncertain whether my letter would reach the Patriarchate. To my delight I received with not too long delay an impressive Greek document signed in ink by the famous Patriarch Athenagoras, inviting me to visit the Holy Mountain under the sole condition that I be bearded, which immediately stopped my daily shaving routine.

I think that, when on my arrival on Mount Athos I was interviewed by the four venerable current executive members of the Holy Synod, the personal invitation by the Patriarch made such an impression on them that, most luckily for me, they overlooked the fact that I was wearing short trousers, as I had nothing more seeming in my rucksack

I augmented my start capital of £25 by selling articles on the political development of Ireland in the course of the first three decades of her independence, to newspapers in Zagreb, Salonica and Istanbul. The editors eagerly accepted my drafts, which I wrote on tables in cafés and taverns, because they welcomed the opportunity to at last be able to publish news of the long forgotten island. In Salonica I became a millionaire when I was paid one and a half million drachmas for two articles! The Irish Times remunerated me a grand total of £40 for all ten instalments of my travelogue.

Throughout the four-month trip I always carried my Kodak Retina Ia camera with me, with which I made a lot of photographs, seven of which illustrated the published series.

While proof-reading the text that resulted from my friend Brian Coleman's dictation from the poorly legible small print of the old dilapidated newspaper cuttings into his computer system, I felt an almost irresistible urge to change my juvenile work by correcting various mistakes, including false facts and the awkward style of writing. I realised, however, that if I started to improve the contents, I would not know where and when to cease destroying the authenticity of my youthful enthusiastic reactions to the encountered experiences. I, therefore, decided to adhere strictly word by word to my original text, including even over- and underpunctuations. The only deviation I permitted myself was to correct the delightful spelling error *gorilla warfare* to *guerrilla warfare*, for which I hold the typesetters responsible!

John S. Joyce, B.E.   Bamberg, Germany   November 2017

This map shows some of the countries through which the writer passed on his journey to Ephesus.

HOW could I realise a four-month stay in the Balkans and in Asia Minor with a travelling allowance of £25—a sum which many consider to be inadequate for a fortnight's stay in Normandy? This was a question I had to answer when I decided on a long-desired touring holiday in South-eastern Europe last June.

TO-DAY we offer the first instalment of " The Road to Ephesus "—the diary of John S. Joyce, which covers his eventful journey made last summer to Turkey. The diary is not only interesting as the record of an ambitious piece of globe-trotting, but also for the penetrating and lively commentary which Mr. Joyce has supplied on the people and places he encountered on his way.

The journey began last June when Mr. Joyce, wih his term examinations in University College, Dublin, successfully completed, found himself with a four-month vacation to fill in. Unabashed by many difficulties, he set out for the south-east of Europe. He travelled as far as Ephesus by the not so simple expedient of hitch-hiking, and returned by the Simplon-Orient express.

John S. Joyce

I

Finance and Compromise

¹ IRISH TIMES, MONDAY, JANUARY 5TH, 1953

¹ HOW COULD I REALISE A FOUR-MONTH STAY IN THE BALKANS AND IN ASIA MINOR WITH THE TRAVELLING ALLOWANCE OF 25 POUNDS—A SUM WHICH MANY CONSIDER TO BE INADEQUATE FOR A FORTNIGHT'S STAY IN NORMANDY? THIS WAS A QUESTION I HAD TO ANSWER WHEN I DECIDED ON A LONG-DESIRED TOURING HOLIDAY IN SOUTH-EASTERN EUROPE LAST JUNE.

Hitch-hiking was the obvious mode of travel to choose in such circumstances. I was full of apprehension as to its workability in S.E. Europe, but now, looking back, such fears seem ridiculous. While in the three countries I toured—Yugo-Slavia, Greece and Turkey—hitch-hiking is completely unknown and traffic is sparse, yet the most essential hitch-hiking requirements are present without which it is doomed to failure, even in the most mechanised countries. These are unbounded hospitality and the desire to help a foreigner to the utmost.

Apprehension turned to conviction of failure on my first contact with Yugo-Slavia, as there was apparently a hopeless scarcity of cars in the country. I soon discovered, however, that hitch-hiking is quite feasible, though it assumes a very different character there than in other countries. One quickly learns that if half-a-dozen vehicles pass in one's direction between sunrise and sundown, then one is on a main artery. The compensation for this alarming lack of traffic is that those who do not respond to the hitch-hiker's thumb sign are in the unimportant minority. Also the traffic is almost exclusively heavy long-distance lorries, and so long lifts are a most welcome feature of hiking through Yugo-Slavia.

Helpful Tourists

The road circulation in Greece is quite dense. I found that the chances of drivers stopping for me where about even. In Yugo-Slav Macedonia I met two French motoring tourists who invited me to accompany them on a ten-day tour of Greece. This very pleasant trip reduced greatly my experience of ordinary hitch-hiking in Greece. In Turkey I became quite a celebrity in the newspapers, in which I was declared to be the first foreign student to practise such travelling in Anatolia. I was instrumental in introducing the word "hitch-hike" into the Turkish language. Unlike most pioneers, I found my task extremely easy. Turkey is very rapidly being developed and there is a heavy traffic (on Balkan standards) of most up-to-date trucks and saloon cars. And the Turks, happily for me, are most interested in foreigners, so I had little walking to do.

The most unusual characteristic of my journey was the succession of buses that helped me. It started in Germany, when, to my surprise, an empty bus stopped. The driver asked me to sit on the floor, lest he be seen taking a passenger while bringing the bus for repairs to Stuttgart. Leaving Sarajevo for the Dalmatian coast, a tourist bus stopped during a mountain storm, though I had not signalled to it. The bus belonged to a well-known English travel agency, who were conducting a party on a tour in Yugo-Slavia. I think the biggest surprise for the score of English occupants of the tour occurred when the thoroughly drenched and capped figure announced his nationality. I travelled in that bus for three days.

*   *   *   *

On going towards Turkey from Salonica I had to traverse the narrow coastal strip of Macedonia and Thrace separating Bulgaria from the Aegean. In this area the last dreadful phases of the civil war were enacted. Today a marked tenseness and military air prevail, and little traffic exists in these war ravaged regions. I anticipated therefore, great difficulty in travelling there. However it took only three days to reach Istanbul from Salonica. For this stage I travelled uniquely in five local buses. Usually it was the police at the many road check points who undertook to help me. The most impressive thing on these journeys was the delighted acceptance of my presence by the passengers. Everybody seemed to take it for granted that a foreigner be given the best seat and be not asked to pay.

The Taxi-bus

But the Turks can reach even greater heights in assisting the poor travelling scholar. Besides the excellent bus services, which are benevolent to foreigners, there are many "dolmushes". A dolmush is best described as a taxi-bus. It is usually in the form of a large current modern American car. The driver operates on a certain route, and only departs when he has filled all seats with passengers. Any time he loses in finding a full load, he makes up for by driving at a reckless speed non-stop to his destination. On several occasions dolmush drivers insisted I take a free place.

The problem of living in these countries I solved by engaging in free-lance journalism. When finances were running dangerously low I used to call at the office of the biggest local daily in the cities I passed through. I found that the editors were very helpful and they often took it upon themselves to entertain me. Articles on Irish events are readily acceptable, as there is a desire to make up the great deficiencies in knowledge about this island. I also wrote explanations of hitch-hiking and about my impressions of the country.

Strange Coincidence

A rather curious language-pun occurred in one of my articles on the political scene in Ireland. In it I described the Taoiseach as being the political giant during the last decades. To my amusement, I found that the Turkish word for giant is "dev"![2]

The beginning of my tour was enjoyable, but uneventful. I went down the Rhine Valley. Heidelberg recorded its greatest temperature since meteorological records have been started, over a century ago. In this heat, it was pleasant to see so much snow along the Grossglockner pass—Austria's premier road-building feat. From the pass it appears to be one steady descent to the Adriatic.

Irish Connection

In Trieste, I was very kindly put up for a couple of days by my namesake, Professor J. Stanislaus Joyce, who came to Trieste with his elder brother, James,[3] and has not left the city since, though he was on the point of being expelled under Mussolini's rule. He is professor of English at the University. He spends most of his

[2] NEW YORK BORN-ÉAMON DE VALERA (1882-1975) DOMINATED IRISH POLITICS FOR DECADES AND BECAME TAOISEACH (PRIME MINISTER) AND SUBSEQUENTLY PRESIDENT OF IRELAND. HE WAS POPULARLY CALLED 'DEV'.

[3] THE FAMOUS IRISH NOVELIST JAMES JOYCE LIVED IN TRIESTE FROM 1904 TO 1915.

spare hours preparing a biography of his brother, which should include several of the late author's yet unpublished essays written in Italian.

II

The Enigma of the West

[1] Irish Times,
Tuesday,
January 6th, 1953

[1] IN A FOUR-WEEK STAY IN YUGO-SLAVIA, I LEARNT THAT SLAV HOSPITALITY AND FONDNESS OF FOREIGNERS IS NO MERE TOURIST BROCHURE CATCH PHRASE. THIS ASPECT OF THE COUNTRY IS GREATLY NEGLECTED. ATTENTION IS FOCUSED ON THE VITUPERATIVE SPEECHES OF YUGO-SLAV LEADERS AND ON THE BRUTAL WORKINGS OF A COMMUNIST STATE TO SUCH AN EXTENT THAT FOREIGNERS ARE INCLINED TO VISUALISE THE YUGO-SLAVS AS A DOUR AND UNWELCOMING RACE.

I think that it is for this reason that the majority of foreign tourists experience a pleasant surprise when they receive such a warm welcome from a vivacious and most amiable people. My journey in the country could be accurately described as one "from household to household". Whether in the country or in the towns, I was invited to stay with families with an unbelievable spontaneity and infallible courtesy.

The Mixing Pot

To talk of a Yugo-Slav is to create a purely political concept. Yugo-Slavia is a federation of six republics containing five vastly different races. While the exterior signs of crossing national frontiers do not exist when going from one republic to another, the essential elements are present—change of race, culture, costumes, and often religion. The country is a veritable mixing-pot of races where Westerns and Orientals meet. The people adhere to the Serbian Orthodox and Roman Catholic Churches, and also to Islam.

A COUNTRY MOSQUE
NEAR JAJCE, IN
TYPICAL ALL-
WOOD BOSNIAN
ARCHITECTURAL STYLE.

The physical aspects of the country are equally varied. In Slovenia rise the ever snow-capped Alps, while Serbia contains an immense fertile plain. The wooded slopes of Herzegovina are not distant from the forbidding barren Karst limestone mountains of Montenegro. Dalmatia has its drought-free river-delta areas, whereas Macedonia bears a semi-desert appearance.

Unhindered Travel

To these stimulating contrasts of races and nature, yet another attraction is today held by Yugo-Slavia for her visitors. It is the only Communist country in the world in which one may talk freely and without being required to prove that one is in accord with the present regime. Few foreign tourists fail to be thrilled by the experience of living in such a novel environment.

To realise her vast projects, Yugo-Slavia is acutely in need of foreign currencies. As in other European countries, to supply this requirement the expansion of the tourist industry is given a high government preference. There is another important reason for the sponsored development of this industry. The Yugo-Slavs feel that they are carrying out a great political experiment and they are anxious that foreigners should come and inspect its operation on the spot. "Putnik" (meaning traveller) offices have been set up in all the important towns. Putnik concerns itself with the least cares of the tourist from hotel reservations to currency exchange. (A characteristic of the cities is that there are no banks.) Rows of attractive polyglots attend to the visitors. Ample documentation is available on all the principal tourist centres.

Tourists Welcome

To encourage foreign tourists, police formalities and form filling have been reduced to a minimum. Police regulations concerning photography are still however very strict and unreasonable. I was arrested once while photographing the picturesque water mills of Bosnia. In the police H.Q. in Sarajevo I was given a polite warning.

It was in that interview that I learned to my surprise how much information the police had about me in their files. The unobtrusive Yugo-Slav police methods should not be interpreted as demonstrating a lack of thoroughness.

Cheap Living

With Spain, Yugo-Slavia must share the distinction of being the cheapest country in Europe for foreign tourists to live in. The Government devalued the dinar by 600% just a year ago. While tourism is being increasingly organised, the disagreeable tourist mentality is not growing amongst the people, who still regard the foreigner as their privileged guest and not as a potential source of easy money.

I found the people extremely intelligent. They show a remarkable quickness in understanding the inadequate efforts of foreigners to express themselves in Serbo-Croat. Long war-time occupation has given many people the legacy of the second language. German is spoken by them with great fluency, and a fair amount of Italian is spoken along the Dalmatian coastline and in Montenegro. French is rarely known outside the Putnik agencies, and English is only recently getting a foothold in the country. Newspapers print lessons in English, where not many years ago they printed similar ones in Russian. There could scarcely be a more significant pointer than this to show in what direction Yugo-Slav sympathy is moving.

Young Population

The youthfulness of the population was one of my first impressions. Everywhere, youths and children looking in excellent health were to be seen, but relatively few elderly people. Many succumbed in war, concentration camps and famines, and others were deported. Such losses are estimated to be one-tenth of the total population. The Communists placed the running of the country in the hands of a young generation, so dispossessing the older ones,. The plight of the elderly people is indeed pitiable, especially of those unable to work, for they are inhumanly neglected.

*   *   *   *

[2] BORN IN CROATIA, JOSIP BROZ TITO RULED YUGOSLAVIA AS A COMMUNIST DICTATOR.

The strength of Tito[2] amongst his subjects is a very tantalising question. No election figures exist to reduce the problem to the simple addition of votes. It can only be guessed from conversations with the people, as in a Gallup Poll. Opinions of observers are bewilderingly contradictory. I am convinced that among the very important youthful section Tito is considered a national hero. Amongst this age group I remarked a spirit of optimism that their lot, though hard at present, is improving. Above all, Tito has satisfied the national xenophobia by his foreign policy. Free from both great camps, the Yugo-Slavs feel strong, and are vastly proud of their unique position in world affairs. Yugo-Slavia, they recognise, is for the first time an international power to be considered. With such feelings, they appear to possess an excellent morale for rebuilding their country.

An atmosphere of extremely hard work pervades. Everywhere huge gangs of workers are to be seen engaged in road building and house construction work. In the summer I saw many youth brigades, comprising students from schools and universities, who devote one month of their vacation to manual work for their country. As is customary in the Balkans, women take very active parts, not only in harvesting, but also in engineering enterprises. The gangs work in peculiar silence; no cement mixer, no pneumatic drill, no bulldozer is to be heard; only the rhythm of shovels, pickaxes and sledge drivers. Women push trucks on rails and carry trays of materials up ramps. These toiling masses are watched over by galaxies of red stars, and they are dwarfed by enormous painted slogans: *Zhivio Tito, Zhivio 1 Mai.*

Life is exceedingly difficult for the people. Inability to work means starvation. Through great effort a worker might earn 5 pounds per month. Black bread costs 4 pence per pound. Clothes and footwear are very expensive and so are well worn and patched before being discarded. Drabness is the keynote of the Yugo-Slav crowds in which it is almost impossible to discern by external appearances the professional man from the labourer. Only the soldiers, sailors and police, who form a very high proportion of the male population, look smart in their Russian-type uniforms and épaulettes.

Colourful costumes

One of the greatest pleasures of travel in Yugo-Slavia is observing the national costumes which are worn daily by both sexes of the rural inhabitants. On Sundays, they are even more numerous and elaborate. I spent one Sunday in the coastal town of Gruda, south of Dubrovnik. There, every woman wore an ankle length white dress with a coloured apron and a large striped sash. Over her shoulders she wore a bolero, finely embroidered with geometrical patterns, and from her neck hung yellow pom-poms. In addition, the married women wore a copious nun-like white head-dress. Weekly, this magnificent theatre-like spectacle may be seen.

The Moslem women in Yugo-Slavia are forbidden to veil themselves. Often, however, I noticed them at my approach raising their arm to conceal the lower portion of their faces! Their menfolk wear white felt egg-shaped skull caps instead of the fez.

Photogenic

Wirelesses, cameras and wristlet watches are at such exorbitant prices that few Yugo-Slavs possess them. My camera always aroused great interest. Children eagerly crowded into my view to be included in photographs. No more appreciated token of thanks for hospitality or other kindness can be given to a benefactor than a photograph of himself.

III

A Fascinating People

[1] Salonica was ablaze with light. Shop windows were illuminated and huge neon signs flickered. Music from packed open-air cafés, casinos and milk bars formed a discordant background to the babble of the well-dressed crowds. This scene surprised me, for after a stay in Yugo-Slavia I ceased to associate such brightness and gaiety with cities. The Yugo-Slav towns are quiet and untouched by American civilisation, whereas the Greek towns bear both contrary features to a marked degree.

[1] IRISH TIMES, WEDNESDAY, JANUARY 7TH, 1953

The sociableness of the Greeks is very impressive. In the country-side no lone farmsteads are to be seen, but many small communities, in which the houses are congestedly arranged as if there were a limitation of the space available for building. Following true Mediterranean fashion, in the cool dusk hours the people promenade up and down the main street dressed in their best attire. Later the men gather in the cafés leaving their womenfolk in similar groups in the houses.

Focal Point

The café is the focal point of Greek life. Over innumerable tiny cups of Turkish coffee and tumblers of freshwater, the men converse. The Greeks derive great pleasure from conversation, and so have brought it to a fine art. They tell stories with great, exaggerated gestures and long, dramatic pauses. I always regretted my inability to understand these discussions. Conversation is not limited to separate table groups, but embraces the whole café, and even passers-by add their views to the topics under discussion. Men shout over the blaring noise from the wireless, inevitably switched on at full volume. The Greeks adore noise, which seems to exercise a stimulating effect on them. As the night advances the cafés become more animated as the occupants sing and dance. They are extremely sober, and no alcohol is required to whip up life among a party of Greeks.

No Strangers

It is in these fascinating cafés that the Greek genius for self-entertainment is best seen. Such gatherings are very democratic. In a single café one may pick out men from all stations in life. Informality is another characteristic of the people. All Greeks seem to know all other Greeks intimately. To the observer, there appears to be no "getting-to-know" stage. No Greek is a stranger in his own country. So sociable are the Greeks that they pitied my lone state. When I explained that I preferred and was in the habit of travelling alone they were completely baffled. To them, enjoyment is almost impossible unless shared by a party of compatriots.

The Greeks are extremely hospitable and most helpful to foreigners. They prefer to entertain a person in a café rather than in their own households. Christian names are exchanged as the preliminary to a conversation and even on the most casual encounter. Then follows a most alarming personal questionnaire regarding age, occupation, single or married, number in the family with corresponding details for each member. These questions one always asked with unfailing Greek courtesy, and to refuse to answer them fully is to be considered churlish. Foreigners at first interpret them erroneously as the probings of an inquisitive mind. Actually they are at the action of a polite person demonstrating his friendship.

Portable Portraits

A Greek carries his most treasured personal belongings in his wallet. It consists of a set of photographs of his family, his acquaintances and himself (if possible in army uniform). After a couple of minutes conversation with a Greek, in which both parties have learnt a lot of personal facts about the other, he very often draws out his wallet and shows his new friend his portable portrait gallery. Sometimes I was pressed to accept a photograph as a momentum! When I was unable to produce a similar collection of pictures, I was regarded with amused interest, made more incomprehensible by my carrying a camera.

A GREEK GENTLEMAN
ENCOUNTERED ON THE
STREETS OF SALONICA.

Hard to Tax

Another characteristic of the Greeks is their individuality. Every
Greek appears to run his own business in his own vague and
seemingly chaotic fashion. I can think of few more unenviable
occupations than that of a Greek tax collector. This national trade
gives Athens one of its most singular features. I never saw in this
bustling modern capital one large general shop, not to speak of

a chain store. Most of the shops and business establishments are small partnerships and family concerns.

The Bigger the Better

Everywhere I was a focal point of attention and the object of prolonged discussion. Crowds would collect around me and from all sides questions would come. My thinness was always remarked and often provoked the anxious enquiry of whether I was hungry. The Greeks carry a healthy percentage of fat and in later years the men without exception display a large paunch; the size often is considered as the criterion of the importance of the bearer. Blue eyes and fair hair they also found strange, but most of all to my surprise, my beard. In Greece, moustaches are universal but the beard is reserved for the priests, monks, recently bereaved and destitute persons. They found it incredible that a person under twenty-one years of age so should wish to grow one. Passing barbershops, I was often assailed by the proprietors. On refusing their services, they sometimes even offered them free of charge! Since the majority of foreign tourists in the country is French, a group of solumn staring children once identified me as a "Pappas Gallos".

*   *   *   *

To most Greeks Irlandia could be in any continent. The name most associated with this island is Shaw[2] who is widely read in the Hellenes. There is a widespread notion that the Irish are a semi-polar race. More than once I was asked whether it were possible in the winter to walk to England!

French is very well established amongst the educated Greeks and it is almost an official language in Athens. The English speaker is rarely at a loss however for in the smallest village in the remotest part, at least one Greek-American is to be found. He usually has been engaged in the catering and restaurant business abroad. I found that often after spending two decades in New York, a Greek could only speak very imperfect English. It appears that even in exile they do not lose their gregarious character and they tend to form tight national communities isolated from the environment of the country. On occasions, I could not understand a single word such a man uttered. Inevitably not a bit crestfallen, he would confidently declare to his admiring friends, "He does not speak English".

[2] GEORGE BERNHARD SHAW (1856-1950), RENOWNED IRISH AUTHOR AND PLAYWRITER.

Tourism is non-existent and travel in Greece is extremely difficult, in spite of the helpfulness of the people. Time is of no import. This attitude frustrates tourists with a set vacation length and ambitious plans to realise.

Greece has survived the ravages of war, occupation, economic chaos and inflation and then civil war only at great cost. Today she is dependent upon foreign aid. The effects of Marshall aid can be seen in every phase of Greek life. The cost of living is soaringly high. Athens is probably Europe's most expensive capital. For one pound note one receives 41,700 drachmas, which only give the dangerous illusion of wealth. There are no coins. 50 drachma notes, worth a fraction more than a farthing, are the size of a 10 shilling note. In practice, notes of less than a thousand drachmas– the price of a cup of coffee, or a newspaper—are little considered, being carelessly rolled up and trust in a pocket. In the cafés and in the banks men are to be seen counting this paper money into million drachma packets.

One Man's Meat

Minarets are not a feature of the Greek landscape. The Greeks are justly proud of having preserved intact their national integrity and heritage during a long Turkish rule. They have, however, adopted an institution from their one-time occupiers that never fails to puzzle and amuse foreigners. It consists of a string of amber beads of varying size, called "koupologi", which Greek men continually finger and swing during their leisure hours. Such beads are to be found also in the near Eastern countries, and they originate from the Moslem prayer beads. I can imagine no better typical souvenir of this fascinating and kindly race than this adult male's plaything.

IV

The Isles of the Aegean

[1] A policeman showed me my sleeping accommodation. It was a clear rectangle on the cobbled courtyard of the Church of Evangelistria, surrounded by hundreds of sleeping figures cramped between their personal belongings and water jars. In common with more than ten thousand pilgrims to the island of Tinos, I had for choice of bivouac the church courtyard or the adjacent fields, and I chose the courtyard.

Tinos is one of the Cyclades group comprising about twenty-four large islands lying between Attica and Crete. I was surprised by the aspect of the Aegean islets. They are arid and treeless, veritable limestone rocks, which make one wonder how the inhabitants survive on such barren ground.

Syros is the capital of the Cyclades. Its port is the only one in the group to have berthing facilities. It was once the biggest Greek port competing with Marseilles and Genoa, until the government started its policy of centralising Athens. Thus Piraeus expanded at the expense of Syros. The main occupation of this beautiful island is today the manufacture of nougat and Turkish delight (loucoums) which is recognised as the best obtainable in the Levant. Confectioners in Athens have long tried to discover the recipe even going as far as importing water from Syros.

Warm Welcome

In all other Cyclades islands, skiffs meet the boat. The calling of a passenger boat is for most islands a weekly event. The watersides are packed with people. All available boats cluster around the ship. Most of them contain just excited sightseers. Passengers scramble up rope ladders and amid great shouting haul up countless baskets without which no Greek seems to travel. To sail from island to island is an exhilarating experience.

[1] IRISH TIMES, SATURDAY, JANUARY 10TH, 1953

Ancient Treasure

Tinos is the largest place of pilgrimage of the Greek Orthodox Church. Over a century ago, an icon, which legend claims St. Luke painted, was found and many miraculous cures where attributed to it. Today it is conserved in a large church to which pilgrims throng annually on the feast of the Assumption. In 1940, on this feast day (August 15th) the Greek cruiser "Elli" while participating in the pilgrimage was torpedoed in the bay by an Italian submarine. This unprovoked act accelerated the war in which the victory of the Greek army over the Italian invaders was popularly attributed to the intercession of Our Lady of Tinos. Since the war, the annual pilgrimages have become very large. This year I was one of the fifteen thousand pilgrims to the island, who swelled its population four fold.

All-day Queue

All day great queues of pilgrims, many of them invalids, waited to kiss the miracle-working icon and to light tapers before it. The church was the richest I saw in Greece. It was filled with icons gilded in most inartistic silver work. The miraculous painting could no longer be seen for the incrustation of precious stones donated by grateful pilgrims. From the hundreds of glittering lamps and the icons hung tokens of thanksgiving. They were mostly metal plates on which were stamped parts of the body in relief attesting to a cure to some limb or organ. Model ships in silver from thankful sailors were suspended from the lamps. A silver model of an antiquated car doubtlessly expressed thanks for the escape from a road accident.

The Swiss of Greece

Mykonos was the next island I visited. The cubistic white town lies in a little bay on the blue Aegean. Small fishing craft line the quaysides. The people of Mykonos could be described as the Swiss of Greece. They keep their houses and streets impeccably white washed so that in the brilliant sunshine they are quite painful to look at. All the houses are flat-roofed and have large unadorned windows. Exterior stone steps mount from the street to the first storeys. The interiors demonstrate the simplicity and warm austerity which characterise the whole island and people. Over this dreamlike town, windmills arrayed on the hills swing slowly their large triangular coloured sails.

The whole island and the town are spotted with churches, which, on a first impression, seem to outnumber the private dwellings. The majority of them are votive chapels which retired sea captains have built in thanks for their deliverance from the perils of the sea. So numerous are they that I once saw a terrace of three such chapels, wall-to-wall, each with its flat campanile. Mass is consecrated only once a year, on the feast day of the saint to whom the chapel is dedicated, in such churches. The people maintain them scrupulously as they do their own homes.

The women of Mykonos weave blankets and scarves from hand spun wool with beautiful patterns consisting of bands of varying thickness of vivid colours. Their gay native costumes include many such shades which are harmonised by the sun. The everyday costume of the women is black which looks very attractive against the white background.

*   *   *   *

Very near to Mykonos is the island of Delos. The ancients considered that this islet occupied the centre of the Cyclades group and it is the legendary birthplace of Apollo and Artemis. The island grew to great importance in the second century before Christ when it was the chief trading port between Europe and the Orient. Such was the sacredness of Delos that no births or burials were allowed to take place on it, the neighbouring island of Rhenea being reserved for such natural occurrences. Today, the ruins of Delos are wonderfully revealed to the visitor through the prodigious labours of the French School of Archaeology. It is uninhabited save for some museum custodians.

Former Glory

The ruins are perhaps the most extensive in Greece, covering the whole island, even to the top of its only eminence. It is difficult to comprehend the enormous prosperity of Delos, whose thousands of inhabitants were totally dependent on imports, since the island itself could not have yielded any resources or agricultural products. In the luxurious merchants' houses, beautiful floor mosaics sparkle in the sun. The system of conserving rain water, a prime worry in the Cyclades, in immense underground cisterns, can be clearly followed. The polished grooves worn into the rims of the cistern heads by the bucket ropes stimulate the imagination.

Spectacular

The most Southern island in the Cyclades is also the most spectacular Aegean island. Santorini is really a volcano submerged in the sea to such a depth that the peak is separated from the crater rim by water; the annular space between them is prevented from being land locked by two breaks, which transform the rim into three islands.

In the centre of the crater, a league in diameter, is the peak which contains the brooding volcano. It is called the "burnt island", for it is covered with massive blocks of jet black lava, like an immense coal stockyard. In the centre burn great fires in areas covered with sparkling moist yellow sulpher crystals. They are so hot that near approach is impossible. The last serious corruption occurred in 1925/6 and a minor one in 1939. Volcanologists believe that another eruption is fast approaching.

Coloured Cliffs

The surrounding islands forming the crater rim rise sheer for more than seven hundred feet. Their cliff faces are streaked with fire-licked strata of volcanic materials contrastingly coloured— black, chocolate, violet and ochre. On top the white line of towns sparkle like icing on a cake. The water in the crater is of the usual ultramarine Aegean colour, with an added peculiar phosphorescence.

It is so deep that ships cannot cast anchor. Many times in the eruptive history of Santorini the water has boiled, and hot water submarine springs always are in action. Fishing boats are often left in certain regions of the bay for a couple of days, where the hot sulphurous water cooks off the barnacles and leaves the hulls clean.

Black Sand

The islands slope gently away from the crater, and end in black sand strands, where the playing children are quite black. The ground is of an off-white volcanic ash, and in this apparently sterile material vines prosper. Their growth is possible during the absolutely rainless six months, due to the clouds of humidity which nightly cover the island. No river, nor a single spring, is to be found, and so the islanders are entirely dependent upon the rain water collected in the cisterns. Water is an expensive item

in the summer. The island is relatively prosperous, for it exports great quantities of raw porcelain to Piraeus, and pumice for the manufacture of hydraulic cement.

Island of Fate

The fate of Santorini lies with the forbidding black island in the centre of the bay. Its fury might cover the islands with another layer of lava, so transforming these idyllic islands for an epoch into silent burnt unearthly land masses. Santorini has been christened the "one black pearl in the Aegean necklace".

V

Land of the Living Dead

¹ IRISH TIMES,
MONDAY,
JANUARY 12TH, 1953

¹ The main preoccupation of foreigners in Greece is inspecting the antiquarian sites. The Greek man-in-the-street expects this enthusiasm of them, but he finds it all rather puzzling. This attitude has been for the most part fostered by foreigners themselves, who have arrived in Greece in national teams to excavate some classical ruin, preferably unaided by other nationalities, to raise the prestige of their own country in the realms of archaeology. Thus Delphi symbolises *"l'oeuvre francaise"*. French, English, Italian, German and American archaeologists have revealed the classical monuments of Greece and built museums to house the precious objects recovered from the soil.

In the museums and the chaotic ruins, foreigners far outnumber the Greeks. Tourist buses disgorge parties of visitors at the walls of ancient cities. Often on an impressively hot humid day these straggling groups of exhausted sight-seers can be seen, mercilessly driven on by pedantic guides. Tourists risk their cars in venturing over some of the most unimaginable mule track roads for the sole purpose of visiting the lone temple of Bassae.

The bewilderment of leisure-loving Greeks at the zealous but rushed pilgrimage of foreigners from ruin to ruin can easily be understood. What are the impulses that drive a quiet businessman and his family on their annual leave to exhaust themselves completely in the mid-summer heat, amid the ruins of the hallowed places of the ancients? The Greeks would be even more perplexed if they heard the oft-repeated declaration of departing tourists: "I never want to see another broken statue or column".

A GREEK PEASANT WOMAN HAND-SPINNING, BELOW A TYPICAL TURKISH-STYLE TIMBER BALCONY, IN THE VILLAGE OF POLIYIROS, IN THE CHALCIDICE PENINSULA.

The Minoan civilisation, the remains of which are best seen in Crete and the later settlements in the Peloponnesus, was one of the best endowed of old times. The Minoans seem to have attached an importance to sanitary arrangements that can only be compared to the modern American ideas. They different radically from the later Greek civilisations in that they adored goddesses, and women were greatly exalted. Frescoes show that women were most active participants in the popular sport of bull baiting. The museum in the Cretan capital, Iraklion, guards all of the *objets d'art* that have been found in the island. In this wonderful museum one can see the most varied and inventive pottery, and the dynamic sculptures of the Minoans, who, besides representing Europe's first civilisation, must also have been one of its most virile and rich.

My tour of Greece was during August and September when the heat was at its severest. From azure blue skies the sun beat down relentlessly, making sunstroke a constant danger. The most disagreeable feature of the Greek climate is the very high humidity. As many Athenians as can during these trying months escape to the mountains or to the Aegean Islands, where refreshing winds continually blow.

The Flute Player

In spite of of the discomfort, I was glad I saw Greece during this period, which, I believe, endows the country with its greatest character. Then the brown earth looks most sterile. In the barren mountains huge flocks of clean sheep and goats raise clouds of white dust. The shephards may be seen standing motionless. They carry tall staffs which always have briar crooks intricately carved into some quaintly grotesque figure. On one occasion, near Olympus, I even heard the famous flute-playing of the lone shepherd at twilight.

All summer, in the fields or in the villages, alone or in gossiping groups, the women peasants are constantly hand-spinning, and they make up the most typical and picturesque scene. They spin exactly as in classical times. On the spike of a staff is secured a mass of teased wool from which they generate a thread. With the right hand they dexterously keep a distaff, on which they wind the thread, rotating in mid-air.

While the summer parches and browns the cracking earth, it fills the villages with colour. Against the house walls lean frames in which strings of tobacco leaves hang and on the balconies and roofs, great yellow Indian corn husks and fruits are laid out. The sun also transforms the grapes of Crete and the Peloponnesus into sultanas and currents. They are spread out on vast areas of canvas. On the gentle slopes of these regions they appear stretched out as great carpets of rich colour.

Were I asked where I saw the most beautiful scenery I would, without hesitation, choose a small area in Thessaly. Kalabaka guards the entrance to the Pindus Mountains, where until recently there was still guerrilla warfare. The approach from the east through semi-fertile undulating country is as unpromising as Kalabaka is startling, for from the hills behind the town surge vertically immense bare mountains of iron limestone. The nearby village of Kastraki can only be reached by canyons through these natural fortifications of rock columns of all sizes.

*   *   *   *

In the late Byzantine period, there were multitudes who wished to escape from the evils of the world. They sought solitude in monasteries situated in the most inaccessible and beautiful parts of Greece. It was natural that they should choose Kalabaka, and on the flat summits of the limestone columns they've founded twenty five monasteries. The only way of reaching these monasteries was to be lifted bodily by a handworked windlass up the three hundred foot high sheer sides.

Dizzy Ascent

Today only five of such monasteries exist, and by the grace of government aid. Greek monasteries are falling in ruins due to the lack of vocations. So wonderful is this Thessaly region, not more than two miles across in its largest dimension, that it has been officially named a tourist locality. Access has been made more easy by the cutting of steps into the rock, so depriving the visitor from his slow, dizzy assent in a basket. Government aid has prevented the surviving monasteries from falling into excessive disrepair, but in all other directions decadence is present.

I planned to spend my first night in this district in the biggest monastery, Varlaam. I followed the difficult path through undergrowth until I came to the base of the rock which bears Varlaam on its lofty top. I then climbed hundreds of steps. The monastery appeared completely abandoned. In the twilight it was frightening to wander through the ill-kept churches, empty cells and storerooms.

In all the other monasteries the largest community is three and they are all of venerable age. These stylites are in acute poverty and are unable to do useful work. The sunset, as seen from these monasteries after a breathless hot day, fills the country with a great tranquillity, and slowly the shadows of the rocks on one another merge into the dark limestone background. It is to be hoped that postulants will come forward and prevent the spectacular and superb Meteora monasteries from falling into final decay.

VI

No children are born on The Mount of Athos

[1] THERE EXISTS IN NORTHERN GREECE A TERRITORY OF ABOUT 120 SQUARE MILES, WHICH, FOR CENTURIES, NO WOMAN OR FEMALE ANIMAL HAS BEEN PERMITTED TO ENTER. IN IMMENSE FORTIFIED MONASTERIES, IN SMALL FARMING COMMUNITIES, IN FISHING VILLAGES, AND IN INACCESSIBLE HOLES IN A MARBLE CLIFF LIVE TWO THOUSAND BEARDED MONKS AND ANCHORITES. THIS REGION, NOT A HUNDRED MILES DISTANCE FROM THE BUSTLING MODERN CITY OF SALONICA, IS A MEDIAEVAL SOCIAL UNIT. IT HAS STUBBORNLY RESISTED ALL CHANGES SINCE ITS FOUNDATION.

[1] IRISH TIMES, TUESDAY, JANUARY 13TH, 1953

Mount Athos, or as it is known in Greece, Agion Oros (Holy Mountain) is the most eastern of the three finger-like peninsulae that protrude into the Aegean from the Chalcidice promontory in Macedonia. In order to manoeuvre his fleet, the Persian king, Xerxes, wished to construct a canal across the isthmus connecting Mount Athos to the mainland. In spite of the prodigious work of slaves, his plan was never realised. Today evidence can be seen of this work in the form of a regular silted valley. Guards patrol here to prevent "women and wolves" from traversing this defile.

From the earliest Christian times, the peninsula was inhabited by ascetics. It was not until the 10th century that these holy men were banded into a community by St Athanasius, who founded the famous monastery of Lavra. From then on monasteries were founded in quick succession. The number of contemplatives rose to thousands. The monasteries were founded and richly endowed by the Byzantine emperors. Later, Mount Athos passed under the jurisdiction of the Ecumenical Patriarch of Constantinople and through adept diplomacy it maintained good relations with the sultans.

Athos received fabulous wealth from the Serbian kings, and also from Russian and other Orthodox rulers. It grew to be a major power in the East. Not only were its monasteries the repositories of unimaginable riches, but it owned nearly all Thrace, Macedonia, great strips in Romania and elsewhere in Central Europe. The power of the peninsula declined with the turn of this century. The great blow came with the Bolshevik revolution, when the majority of the overseas lands and investments where irretrievably lost.

Came Autonomy

Today Mont Athos possesses no extraterritorial property, and so is made dependent upon its own meagre resources. In 1878 the autonomy of the Holy Mountain was recognised internationally in the Treaty of Berlin. Its status vis-à-vis the Greek monarchy was settled by treaty in 1927, when a constitution based on nine centuries of precedent was drawn up.

The majority of the monks belong to the Greek Orthodox Church, but there are also about 400 Russian Orthodox monks. The Serbian, Bulgarian and Romanian Orthodox Churches are also well represented. The constitution stipulates that all members of the Athos community must be Greek subjects, irrespective of their previous nationalities. Like all the clergy in Greece, they are exempted from compulsory military service, but they are disenfranchised in the national and local elections.

Medieval Pattern

The government of this theocracy follows a mediaeval pattern. In the capital, Karyes, sits a legislative body, the Holy Synod, composed of twenty representatives drawn from each of the score of ruling monasteries. This number has been carefully fixed. Russia made great efforts to bring this Aegean unit into her power. Vast sums of money were expended to build Russian monasteries. The Patriarch, alarmed at this threat to the Hellenism of the peninsula, limited by an edict the number of ruling monasteries to twenty. Of them only one each went to the Russian, Serbian and Bulgar factions. Even when the Russians far outnumbered the Greeks in the territory, they only commanded one vote in the Central Assembly, whereas the Greeks had seventeen votes at their disposal. Each representative is elected annually by the elders of his monastery.

THE MONASTERY OF SIMOPETRA, HIGH ON MT. ATHOS. IN SPITE OF ITS VAST SIZE, IT HOUSES ONLY 45 MONKS. THERE ARE ELEVEN STOREYS IN ALL—THE FOUR LOWER ONES HAVE ONLY TINY WINDOWS AND ARE USED AS STORES. THE MONASTERY HAS BEEN TWICE BURNED DOWN AND REBUILT. THERE WERE NO SURVIVORS OF EITHER FIRE.

The executive power is held by four members of the Holy Synod, who form the Holy Epistasia. The monasteries are divided into tetrades of four each. These tetrades become, for one year, on a rota, the Holy Epistasia. The representative of the principal monastery in the Holy Epistasia is the Protepistates—the constitutional head of the Holy Community of Mount Athos.

Difficult to Enter

Entry into Mount Athos, while being impossible for a woman, is difficult for a man due to its isolation and to the formalities required. It is advisable to procure letters of introduction from members of the Greek Orthodox Hierarchy. It is essential to obtain a visa from the Greek Ministry of Foreign Affairs, as, due to the special jurisdiction of Mount Athos, a tourist visa for Greece does not suffice. The Royal Hellenic Ministry will consider an application for a visa only when it is accompanied by an official request from the diplomatic representative of the applicant's country. The British Embassy authorities kindly provided me with the necessary flamboyant *Note Verbale* in the absence of diplomatic relations between Ireland and Greece.

There are two ways of reaching Mount Athos from Salonica.

The first involves at least a whole day trip in a caique to the port of Athos - Daphni. The second is along the ill-maintained road that passes through the most picturesque country before reaching Ierissos, the last Greek village before the isthmus. This village is known for its preponderance of women since their menfolk earn their living in the adjacent holy territory.

*   *   *   *

On arrival at one of the monastery ports there is an interview by the Greek police, who, by treaty right, maintain half-a-dozen small garrisons in Mount Athos. They check passports and papers and direct the stranger to reach Karyes as as soon as possible. The capital is big. It is surrounded by great turnip-shaped domes of Russian buildings. The usual town establishments are run by both monks and laymen. An air of laziness and inactivity prevails. Nowhere else in Athos is the absence of women so noticeable. For over ten centuries no woman has given birth to a child in this town. No children play in the streets.

The visitor is first obliged to call on the Greek Governor-General and then to the chief of police, who gives in exchange for the visa and passport a slip of paper. Without this paper audience with the Holy Epistasia is impossible.

Monastic guards, resembling the Pontifical guards in the Vatican, lead one to the Holy Epistasia. They are dressed in long black cloaks and shiny black cylindrical hats without any insignia or ornaments testifying their exalted positions. They examine carefully the introductions. Fortunately, I had one from the Patriarch, under whose authority Mount Athos lies, as well as from the Metropolitan of Salonica, which appeared to give me added prestige. On the approval of the four venerable bearded members, a *Diamonitirion* is made out. It is a typed formal letter to all the monasteries, and on it is inserted the visitor's name, his introducers' names and the purpose of his visit. The *Diamonitirion* orders the monasteries to extend to the bearer all possible hospitality and facilities for the realisation of his object of visit as specified. It is signed by the four members and stamped with the four-part seal of the Holy Community.

"On the House"

Such is the world famous hospitality of the Holy Mountain, that for food or sleeping accommodation there is never a request for payment. I never once saw a receptacle where one might place a discreet offering. The cafés and restaurants of Karyes are the only places where one may eat *à la carte* and be presented with a bill. Less than a thousand *Diamonitirions* were issued to both Greek and foreign visitors during the whole of 1951. Greeks experience considerably more difficulty in obtaining one than foreigners. It is assumed that the latter do not come purely to benefit from the magnificent Athonite hospitality.

The mediaeval atmosphere has been conserved by excluding modern scientific inventions as far as possible. A formidable silence reigns over the peninsula. There are no wheeled vehicles. No petrol engine is to be heard save for the "putt-putt" of a *benzina* chugging from one monastery port to another. The cinema is non-existent. The majority of the ruling monasteries are connected directly to Karyes by telephone. While the monks greatly long for electricity, there is only one monastery, Vatopedi, that possesses a supply. Sleep is difficult in this monastery, due to the monotonous throb of Athos' only diesel plant placed below the guest rooms.

Time is Elastic

Vatopedi shows modernisation in other directions. It is the only monastery to adhere to the Gregorian calendar and Greek time. Elsewhere on the peninsula Byzantine time is used. It involves putting the clock to midnight when the sun sets, hence it is variable. Three o'clock in the afternoon means that there are nine hours to sunset. At midnight Byzantine, the entrances to all the monasteries are barred. No system of hour counting could instil the easy going monks of Athos with time consciousness. The monasteries follow the Justinian calendar, which is thirteen days in retard of the modern calendar. My first day I spent in Vatopedi, and such was the length of my stay in Mount Athos, that when I left it from the harbour of St. Pantaleimon monastery, the calendar showed the same day as when I entered this unique world.

VII

I meet the Russian Hermits—and talk about St. Kevin

[1] IRISH TIMES, WEDNESDAY, JANUARY 14TH, 1953

[1] TWO THOUSAND MONKS LIVE IN THE WOMANLESS COMMUNITY OF MOUNT ATHOS. THEY ALL WEAR LONG BLACK CLOAKS AND HARD, BLACK CYLINDRICAL HATS. FROM THEIR DAY OF ENTRY INTO THE CELIBATE COMMUNITY THEY ARE NOT ALLOWED TO SHAVE OR TO CUT THEIR HAIR, BUT THEY TIE IT INTO A LARGE BUN. TO THE CASUAL OBSERVER, THESE THOUSANDS OF UNIFORMLY BLACK-GARBED, BEARDED MONKS GIVE THE IMPRESSION OF HOMOGENEITY IN ATHONITE LIFE. THIS COULD NOT BE FURTHER FROM THE TRUTH. MANY TYPES OF MONASTIC SYSTEMS AND UNITS EXIST.

There are only twenty monasteries represented in the Government of the peninsula. The majority of the monks do not live in these ruling monasteries, but in smaller communities. The constitution lays down that only the ruling monasteries may own property. Thus all the other monastic buildings and lands are the property of some ruling monastery and their occupants dependents of it. The dependent monastic settlements are called skitae, kellia, kalyvae and ichikastiria.

A skete is best defined as a monastery with no voice at the capital Karyes. It is taxed by and subordinated to its ruling monastery. It is normal to have about thirty monks in a skete. They are usually poorer and work harder as farmers or fishermen than the monks of ruling monasteries. A kellion is normally occupied by three monks. They earn their living by engaging in handicrafts, most commonly wood sculpture, icon painting or rug weaving. The size of the garden is limited so that it only supplies some meagre necessities.

A kalyva has neither a chapel nor a garden and it usually houses one or two hermits. The only amenity such a dwelling is allowed to possess is a rain water system. The hermit earns a pitiable living from the products of some painstaking craft. The ichikastiria is reserved for the most fanatical of Athos inhabitants, who renounce their fellow-creatures forever. It consists simply of a cavity in the marble landslide in which Mount Athos ends. They are placed like the nests of sea birds.

The anchorite commences his tenure by being lowered by rope and windlass into his inaccessible habitation. At long, regular intervals, the ruling monastery undertakes to lower necessary provisions to the ascetic hermit. When the contents of the basket remain untouched preparations are started for monks to descend into the cave and remove the corpse for interment.

No Females

For centuries female insects and birds have been the only creatures to have violated the constitutional exclusion of the female sex. There are, naturally, many stories of the intrusion of women into the peninsula, but none of them have been proved. The most elaborate methods have always been employed to enforce this ban.

There has, however, always been a tendency towards laxity in the prohibition of female animals. The poorer skitae were often unable to resist the huge prices obtainable from the elders of richer monasteries for a fresh egg. They, therefore, engaged clandestinely in poultry-keeping. So bad became these abuses that in 1926 the Patriarch ordered the systematic slaughter of all hens on the Holy Mountain. A few years ago a relaxation was authorised; hens may now be kept by the monasteries outside the Walls, so dealing a death-blow to the fabled Athonite stale egg! But, alas, I was scandalised one day to see in a skete some forbidden ducks.

Great numbers of miserable cats are kept in each monastery to keep the rats and mice at bay. Male bonhams are imported and reared by the monks. The beasts of burden and transport are mules and jack asses.

Month-Old Bread

The visitor to Mount Athos is put on the same diet as the monks, who are strictly vegetarian. The Athonite bread is made at intervals of about a month. It is suspended in baskets from the kitchen ceilings to prevent rats from attacking it. It is the hardest and blackest imaginable. Since most of the monks are very old, they usually tear out what is between the crusts, and soak it in a large pewter jug of wine, while the long grace preceding meals is recited. For vegetarians, the monks have a surprisingly high alcoholic consumption. Their ration is over a pint per day of excellent wine, and an equal quantity of *ouzo* (aniseed spirit) per week.

One is continually served up with every member of the bean family submerged in tepid oil. Giant tomatoes, onions, garlic, olives, fish, cheese and fruit are the most common foods. I was fortunate in the season I was with the monks, for when I was not satisfied with the monastery meals, I had only to go out and help myself from the bountiful harvest of nuts and grapes. The monks kindly ignored my protracted sorties into their vineyards.

The Holy Community take particular pride in using the most ancient conventions and implements. An example of this is the "simandra" which never fails to fascinate strangers. The simandra consists of a long baulk of hardened wood, which is suspended horizontally and may be struck with a mallet. This instrument was used long before the bell in Christian communities. It symbolises Noah's calling of the animals into the safety of the ark. The monk striking the simandra produces a savage rhythm of ascending frequency, culminating in three tremendous imperative blows.

Wealthy Fortresses

The monasteries of Athos are built upon a grandiose scale, usually near or projecting over the sea. They are essentially fortifications, for they have always been the objects of attack by raiders for their great wealth. They present crennelated towers and unscalable walls to the exterior. High up on the walls jut out wooden balconies supported on curved timber struts. These walls enclose a courtyard, which can only be reached by a single vaulted passage entrance through them.

The refectories are the most curious buildings in Athos. In Lavra and Vatopedi, the scores of tables and benches are hewn out of marble. Around the side of each table runs a groove to channel away the spilt oil, wine and soup. Large holes are bored in the centre to contain the condiments. To witness an Athonite community partaking of a meal is a mediaeval and most extraordinary sight which no child learning table etiquette should be allowed to watch.

Fire Takes Toll

The buildings are often of much more recent origin than one would at first imagine. The fire destruction in Athos is appalling. Usually the only original part of the monastery, dating from its foundation, are the all stone fortified towers and the courtyard catholicon.[2] The remaining parts are often built at the end of the last century. To avoid further damage to them, the fabulous vestments, treasuries and library are conserved in the tower and the innumerable precious relics of each monastery in the catholicon.

[2] MAIN CHURCH OF EACH MONASTERY, ALWAYS SITUATED AS A SOLITARY BUILDING IN THE CENTRE OF THE COURTYARD.

To visit the library is often most difficult. Three monks must assemble to open it. Shelves are packed tight with early byzantine manuscripts. One can take down and finger through 9th and 10th century New and Old Testaments from Constantinople. In a monastery which possesses one of the worlds most important collections of byzantine manuscripts, the librarian confessed to me that he was semi-illiterate.

Russian Hermits

The mile and a quarter high peak of Athos Mountain is less than three miles distant from the end of the peninsula. The impression on seeing the majestic pyramid profile of the mountain is that a greater portion of it has crashed into the sea, creating Europe's greatest landslide. On these precipitous marble regions live Athos' most interesting ascetic inhabitants.

I was advised to visit Papa Nikon in the Russian hermit settlement of Karoulia. Karoulia is, I discovered, a conglomeration of tiny abodes, kalyvae, worked into the almost vertical portions of the cliff. The Russian hermits gave me the usual jolly reception. They insisted that I should accept a meal. They prepared a large wooden bowl of their national "bortsch", but without pork, and great cups of weak Russian tea.

TWO HERMITS OF A KELLION IN ST. BASIL'S SETTLEMENT BESIDE THEIR BONE CRYPT. THE SKULLS ARE THOSE OF THEIR PREDECESSORS, AND EACH ONE BEARS THE NAME NEATLY INSCRIBED.

My hosts volunteered to lead me to Papa Nikon. They were all of venerable age, with long flowing grey beards. In a city, such men would be expected to ask younger people to help them to cross the street. I was to learn to respect their agility

The journey involved crossing vertical rock faces by the aid of heavy chains slung across them. Trembling, with my face to the rock, I felt for foot grips while I clung desperately to the chain. My fear increased when I saw the profoundly deep Aegean far away down below me. I was handicapped by a knapsack and nailed boots that were treacherous on marble.

The performance of my septuagenarian guides was truly astonishing, and has left an indelible impression on my mind. With monkey-like rapidity of movements, and a nonchalance as if they were walking on *terra firma*, their beards blown over their shoulders by the wind, they crossed the rock walls.

St. Kevin

Moscow-born Papa Nikon greeted us warmly in his tiny cave dwelling. He was small and thin with a wrinkled face and patchy beard. Before entering the contemplative life he had travelled throughout the continents. With his national linguistic talent, he learned languages quickly and speaks nine fluently. His English is flawless. In spite of living in Mount Athos for over two decades, he appeared to know less Greek that I had picked up in six weeks. This fact demonstrates the isolation of the different communities in Athos and the enmity between the Russian and Greek monks.

Papa Nikon was delighted I was Irish. He immediately asked me did I know "Glendaloo". He was charmed to learn the correct pronunciation. He had read a lot about his Irish anchorite counterpart, St. Kevin,[3] and on medieval Irish monasticism. He begged me to send him some pictures of the seven churches. This conversation reminded me how closely St. Kevin's bed resembles many Athonite abodes.

[3] ST. KEVIN (498-618), FAMOUS IRISH SAINT AND FOUNDER ABBOT OF GLENDALOUGH MONASTERY. HE LIVED ALONE AS A HERMIT IN A NEARBY CAVE.

Decadence and senility of the overall impressions of Mount Athos. At two thousand, the monks are at half their pre-war strength. Many kellia are abandoned. Only a hundred decrepit monks live in vast St. Pantaleimon Monastery which once held eighteen hundred. A young monk is so exceptional as to be instantly noticed. Almost all the beards on Athos are gray. Even the postulants are at an advanced age. They give the impression that they are really old men who wish to withdraw from the struggle of life to the peacefulness of Mount Athos. The intellectual life, which at one time must have been intense, is dead. One cannot help feeling that Mount Athos is fast approaching a cataclysm, when this last mediaeval world will be flooded with modernism.

VIII

Turks are curious but full of hospitality

[1] ANY VISITOR TO TURKEY WHO EXPECTS TO FIND THE COUNTRY INHABITED BY SMALL, SWARTHY, PIRATICAL-LOOKING PEOPLE, WEARING CRESCENT EAR-RINGS AND CARRYING FLASHING SABRES, IS QUICKLY DISABUSED OF SUCH IDEAS. THIS DISAPPOINTMENT IS AS SURE AS WITH PEOPLE WHO VISUALISE THE IRISH AS ARMED WITH SHILLELAGHS AND IN CONSTANT COMMUNICATION WITH THE FAIRIES.

[1] IRISH TIMES, THURSDAY, JANUARY 15TH, 1953

As I watched Turkish workmen hurriedly drinking their morning coffee before going to work, I often felt that the scene was quite familiar to one in an English transport café. The Istanbul crowds have little to distinguish them from those in Western European capitals. To choose the typical Turk would be well-nigh impossible. There are many different races that answer to the name "Turkish".

I spent almost a month in the country. As with the Balkan people I travelled amongst, I have nothing but praise for the wonderful hospitality and kindness of the Turks.

The majority of visitors visit Istanbul, but do not venture outside its immediate environs. Izmir is the only other city to receive a sizeable number of tourists. These usually have made it a port of call in a Mediterranean cruise. The rest of the vast country is virtually unvisited by foreigners, excepting Ankara, which houses a world of foreign commercial and diplomatic officials.

The Turks of Anatolia are much more unused to foreigners than the Greeks. This isolation, and the Oriental idleness of the men, who leave all the back-breaking toil to their wives and daughters, are, I think, the main factors to cause the incredible curiosity of the Turks.

Security-Conscious

Everywhere I went, pairs of eyes held me in their fixed and undisguised gaze. As I passed, people stopped, and sometimes changed their direction of walking to observe me further. It was not uncommon in the towns for the police to intervene to disperse the crowds that would cluster around me.

I was continually questioned. The Turks are very often very security-conscious. They sometimes called a *gendarme* to examine my credentials. Once they are satisfied that you are a sightseer, their only worry is how to help you to the utmost.

OFTEN WHEN I HAD FINISHED THE FIRST ITEM I HAD ASKED FOR IN A RESTAURANT, THE WAITER WOULD PLACE BEFORE ME AN UNORDERED DISH. WHEN I LOOKED UP INQUIRINGLY, I WOULD ALWAYS SEE A MAN AT ANOTHER TABLE BEAMING WITH SMILES.

These graceful discreet gifts are often most unenjoyable. Turkish delicacies are frequently horrible tasting concoctions to an Irish palate. The only reward the benefactor wished was to see my enjoyment, so it had to be swallowed with a smile!

The fact that one is never invited into the people's homes should not be interpreted as a lack of hospitality. Turkey is a purely Moslem country. Despite its modernisation, the seclusion of women is still a strong social convention.

Alms

The overwhelming kindness that Turks extend to foreigners is well illustrated in an amusing incident that happened me. One night in the town of Kayseri, which occupies the centre of the Anatolian plain, I was looking for overnight accommodation. A hotel keeper wanted two Turkish liras (about five shillings). I had never paid more than half this sum for a bed in Turkey. I argued that, as I was a student, he should allow me a reduction.

In the room there were about a dozen men seated drinking tea and coffee, while taking a profound interest in everybody else's business. I became aware of coins being rattled among this group and of muffled words being said. When I turned around I saw one of the men with an outstretched hand. His colleagues were dropping coins on to his palm, while quietly saying "Allah", as all Moslems do when they give alms. My bargaining had prompted them to subscribe to my expenses.

I was both amused and greatly impressed by this spontaneous act. As best I could, I thanked them heartily explaining that being a student I had some money, but not a lot. I departed as they were excitedly arguing how much should be returned to each man by the collector.

As I was walking down the street about six of the men came rushing after me. With much good humour they led me back to the hotel. The hotelier entered my passport details into the register. To everybody's great pleasure, he would not now hear of my paying a single coin for my board!

From my knowledge of the Turks, I can reconstruct what must have happened in my few minutes absence. *En masse*, the men must have reproached the hotel-keeper for his "incivility" towards me, a foreigner. They must have reflected on the bad feelings I might entertain as a result towards Kayseri. To make amends for his lapse in courtesy, he evidently declared he would put me up free.

French Spoken

In Istanbul there are rarely any language difficulties. French is almost universally spoken. This is due to the many French *lycées* that were founded by priests who had been expelled during the anti-clerical period in France. These are now the preferred schools in Istanbul. English is fairly widespread among the young people, especially in Ankara. There is a very large population of Greeks in Istanbul and Izmir, but not elsewhere in the country. Anyone who wishes to travel in Anatolia must make great efforts to learn Turkish. The chance of meeting a Turk there who knows a foreign language is so unlikely that it may be discounted.

As in Greece, the café is the hub of Turkish social life. All day long the cafés are filled with chatting men, who leisurely sip tiny cups of strong Turkish coffee or small tumblers of sweet herb tea. They smoke unceasingly. Cigarettes are almost at a nominal price.

The Turkish hookah has not gone out of fashion. It is called a *nargile*. It consists of a glass bowl with a long narrow neck, on which rests a brazier containing tobacco and a red ember. A pipe leads from the burner down the neck to below the water level. To the top of the bowl is attached a very long flexible pipe, that ends in the monstrously large amber mouthpiece with a woolly hand grip on it. The nargile is usually placed on the café table. The strong pull exerted by the smoker bubbles the smoke up through the water and conducts it up the twisting tube to his mouth. The quiet nargile smokers, often in groups, never failed to fascinate me.

The Turks have a very strong nationalist feeling. Sometimes it will prevent them from listening to any criticisms of their country. There is a deep popular feeling for their great reformer, Mustafa Kemal Ataturk.

THEY HAVE AN ALMOST FANATICAL HATRED OF THE RUSSIANS. THEIR COUNTRY'S VERY STRONG STAND WITH THE WEST IS, I THINK, MORE ATTRIBUTABLE TO THIS THAN TO A VIOLENT ANTI-COMMUNIST SENTIMENT.

The Veil

A common cliché used abroad to describe Ataturk's reforms in his country is: "He abolished the veil". This shows an inadequate appreciation of the difficulties in overthrowing ancient institutions. It is true that in the large cities, the women follow the Parisian modes rather than the fashions of their mothers. However, thirty years is not sufficient to break down the old customs of the peasantry. In all the villages, the women wear the same shapeless black gowns and headdress, which they pull over their faces on the approach of a man. In the more isolated regions they go permanently veiled. The girls attending school are compelled to wear a uniform that would not look strange on Irish schoolgirls.

The reform in men's clothing has been more successful. The fez has been replaced by the Western hat in the cities and by the cloth cap in the country. Other garments are also quite westernised. The Turkish baggy trousers have been incorporated into the Western design of trousers in many regions of Anatolia.

Ataturk's rule was extremely anti-clerical. Today no priest, whether Moslem, Orthodox or Catholic, may appear in public in clothes that indicate his religious vocation. Religion as a life-force in the country has disappeared. Only recently the law that no Christian could hold an army commission has been withdrawn.

It is considered non-progressive to attend the mosques. It is a sad sight to see the vast floor spaces of the Istanbul mosques accommodating a few dozen people about the mihrab. The fez the Imam wears within the mosque walls was the only one I saw worn in the whole country.

The men usually turn their cap peaks to the back of their head so as to comply with two necessary conditions for prayer: the head must be covered and the forehead touch the ground. The muezzin still calls the faithful to prayer five times a day from the lofty balconies on the tall, slender, pencil-like minaret. I doubt if ever before his cry was so much in vain.

IX

The Cone-Country of Cappadocia

[1] Throughout an area the size of County Dublin, in Central Turkey, nature can be seen in one of her most wonderous and eccentric moods. This region, in the province of Cappadocia, is covered with hundreds of thousands of the most bizarre forms in volcanic pumice rock-pillars, cones, pyramids, turrets and ridges. Some are formed with geometrical perfection, others are chaotic masses that defy description. The ensemble forms a fantasy resembling, perhaps, a lunar landscape.

[1] IRISH TIMES, FRIDAY, JANUARY 16TH, 1953

The cone country of Cappadocia lies on a parallel with the toe of Italy and has the same longitude as Jerusalem. It is situated near the town of Kayseri which is dominated by the ever snow-capped extinct volcano of Erciyash Dagi. Being responsible for the creation of the adjacent geological phenomenon it is the "Father of the Cones".

Millenniums ago this lofty volcano covered an approximately triangular area with volcanic ash often hundreds of feet deep. On top was added in places a thin layer of lava or pumice. As this fiery mass cooled it contracted and it was rent with great cracks. For centuries rain and snow ran through these fissures on the way to the Kizilirmac river. The lava had good resistance to the flow of water, but the underlying volcanic material was rapidly eroded, so that the gullies grew bigger and bigger.

Nature's Dual Part

Today, the water has receded, leaving the area serrated with numerous parallel valleys or dried up river beds. The rocks are arrayed at various heights along the valley slopes and bed. They are traversed by bands of slightly different colour and texture. In all the formations the corresponding bands are the same height or run along the line oblique to the ground. They are the strata of the volcanic deposits. From this effect it can be seen clearly that all the formations once belonged to the same great homogenous mass.

But the scene is not static as the wind continues to erode the country. Those rock shapes which are topped by slabs of invulnerable lava are protected against this action. There are immense areas in smooth furrows which reminded me of sheep huddled closely in a fold. These are really cones in the making; for the erosive action of the wind is continually shaping and cutting them apart. Thus the dual role of nature as creator and destroyer is once again evident.

Many of the rocks resemble animals, and are appropriately named. Those capped with dark lava blocks have often a most distinctive look. They wear their caps frequently at a rakish angle or a coquettish slant. The countryside is not altogether monochrome, though chalk and grey predominate. There are also yellow, blue and rose, with intermediate light subtle shades. There are areas of definite colourings and similar shapes.

I saw fields of cones like some bellicose army encampment, and clusters of columns as in a ruined temple. I was fortunate to be in this district at a full moon period. Under its light and with the prevailing silence, these white rocks appear as ghostly shapes lacking all substance.

FROM THE FIRST CENTURY ONWARDS, CAPPADOCIA WAS THE CHOSEN REFUGE OF CHRISTIAN CONTEMPLATIVES. HUGE AREAS OF THE EASILY-WORKED ROCK WERE HONEYCOMBED WITH HERMIT SETTLEMENTS. THE VALLEY OF GÖREME ALONE HAS MORE THAN A THOUSAND ROCK CHURCHES.

The countless apertures, leading to oratories and cells pitted in the rocks, now lie gaping and vacant. They give an inexpressible atmosphere of desolation and accursedness to this valley.

The number of Cappadocian hermits is said to have been twenty thousand. I, at first, estimated far more than that number, as I gazed at the countless thousands of habitations over large areas resembling the nests of sand martins. Cave dwellers usually prefer to scrape out a new abode rather than to live in a recently vacated one. At no time in the twelve centuries of Cappadocian monastic history would more than a fraction of the existing caves have been inhabited simultaneously.

THE FANTASTIC
LANDSCAPE IN THE
CAPPADOCIAN "CONE-
COUNTRY".

Refuge for Hermits

It is clear that each anchorite or community of monks chose a
certain rock in which to hew out their chapels and cells. The
layout of these recluses show concern for protection against plund-
erers. Often the entrance is near the top of a cone, so that when
the rope ladder or rope is withdrawn entry is impossible. In such
cases the ascetics built downwards in the rock.

Many have their entrances at a more rational height, but in
these dwellings the chapel and most important chambers are on
the top storeys. These can only be reached by a steep stairway,
and through a hole in the floor of the uppermost level. This hole
could be blocked securely by rolling a great stone over it.

DOUBTLESSLY THESE STYLELITES MUST OFTEN HAVE BEEN BES-
IEGED BY BANDITS IN THEIR NATURAL IMPREGNABLE ROCK FORT-
RESSES FOR LONG PERIODS. THERE IS ONE RIDGE WHICH HAS
AS MANY AS SIXTEEN STOREYS OF MONASTIC APARTMENTS CUT
IN IT.

Interesting Churches

The churches are of great interest. Due to the isolation of Cappadocia, there has been negligible research done in this most promis-

ing field. Their entrances are usually in the form of simple inset facades, showing strong Egyptian influence. The interiors are very small and are built on the conventional Byzantine plan. The iconostasis and altar are carved directly out of the rock.

Those dating from about the second and third centuries show signs of primitive interior decoration. Those from the eighth century onwards have their entire interior walls and cupolas covered with magnificent frescoes painted directly on the chipped rock face. The physical conditions for the preservation of these priceless examples of early Byzantine iconography are ideal, but vandals have frequently destroyed and disfigured these images by cutting lines in the soft rock.

Many chapels were built during the iconoclastic controversy. They have only lines of Maltese crosses and geometric designs for interior adornment. There are many catacomb-like crypts and innumerable cells, inter-connected by tiny three-foot high passages. The benches and tables in the vast refectories are of one piece with the rock.

BUT CAPPADOCIA DOES NOT BELONG ENTIRELY TO THE PAST. NOT A SINGLE CHRISTIAN SURVIVES IN THIS ERSTWHILE CHRISTIAN STRONGHOLD.

The Turkish population live mostly on the export of pumice material and vine-growing. As on the island of Santorini, no real soil exists, but only off-white friable volcanic material. This unpromising substance is fertilised for viticulture by the addition of guano. The inhabitants have partially walled up countless caves, and even superb chapels, to transform them into dove-cotes. Annually the life-giving guano of the sky-darkening flights of doves is harvested.

Pumice Villages

The contemporary villages are most fascinating. A typical house has an arcaded facade of pumice blocks. Behind it, scraped out of the rock on a single level, stretch rooms, stores and stables for donkeys, which provide the only means of transport in this region.

I LIVED FOR TWO DAYS IN THE VERITABLE LOST VILLAGE OF AVCILAR. IT IS BUILT IN A FOREST OF GREAT ROCKS LIKE PENCIL STUBS. ITS MAIN STREET IS A DRIED-UP RIVER BED COVERED WITH FINE WHITE SAND RIPPLED BY THE WIND.

The reforms of Ataturk do not seem to have reached this remote part. The women are veiled and wear shawls of brightly coloured striped material. They lead a most secluded existence. The stranger is observed discreetly by eyes peeping from holes near the tops of their fantastic cone dwellings.

The young girls wear their long hair in about a dozen thin plaites. They darken their eyes and hands with henna. The men dress in large baggy trousers and great white sashes. The muezzins call the faithful from their natural pumice minarets. I cannot imagine any village bearing a more astonishing aspect.

Were it not situated in such an inaccessible spot, the cone-land of Cappadocia would certainly, and most deservedly, become an international household word, like the Grand Canyon or the Giant's Causeway. Not only is it, like them, a wonderful geological phenomenon, but it also enshrines a most valuable museum of Byzantinee mysticism and many most extraordinary semi-troglodyte villages.

No tourist facilities exist in the area, and the rare visitor is left to his own resources. As I climbed up rock sides or crawled through holes to inspect chapel wall frescoes or crypt interiors I enjoyed that real sense of discovery that is so often lacking in recognised tourist localities.

I COUNT THIS AS BY FAR THE MOST SPECTACULAR AND INTER-ESTING PLACE I VISITED DURING MY WHOLE TOUR. WITH THE INCREASING FACILITIES OF MODERN TRAVEL AND THE WESTERN-ISATION OF TURKEY, THE CONE COUNTRY OF CAPPADOCIA CAN-NOT LONG REMAIN OUT OF THE LIMELIGHT OF WORLD RENOWN.

X

Ephesus at last—and home again

[1] IRISH TIMES,
SATURDAY,
JANUARY 17TH, 1953

[1] To anyone who has come from the Anatolian plain, Western Turkey appears to be most luxuriant. The former possesses a certain grandeur, despite its monotony. It's brown, gently undulating and treeless terrain gives the impression of limitless space.

The Anatolian population live in widely scattered poor villages constructed of mud. At a distance it is hard to discern these mud villages, as they provide no contrast in colour with their background. The Aegean seaboard, however, is more sharply cut by valleys, and the mountains are densely wooded.

The villages, of all timber construction, have a considerably more prosperous aspect than those in the interior.

Izmir is today Turkey's largest export port. Through it are sent the products of the rich hinterland. The small sleepy town of Selchuk lies midway between Izmir and the River Menderes. The English word "meander" is derived from this river, which follows an extremely tortuous course. Wooded hills protect flat valley beds, in which prosper cotton plantations and enormous fig groves. From these trees originate the world-famous Symrna dried figs. Trains of camels, led by a man seated on an ass, lumber disdainfully through the streets of Selchuk burdened with great bursting sacks of raw cotton.

It is hard to believe that at such an unimportant town is the successor of Ephesus. From the eleventh century before Christ until the fifteenth century, Ephesus was the biggest port of Asia Minor and a world centre of culture. Next to Jerusalem, Ephesus is, perhaps, the second holiest Christian city.

It is a most important archaeological site, for it has handed down magnificent monuments of all the main epochs of its three millennium past—Persian, Greek, Roman, Byzantine, Seljuk and Ottoman. Each succeeding civilisation did not hesitate to despoil the buildings of past generations to construct new edifices. In many walls and in the great aqueduct great marble columns and pieces of statuary have been employed as construction materials.

Diana

Before the coming of Christianity, Ephesus was the centre of the great cult of Diana. To her was built, and rebuilt seven times, a superb temple. It was the largest temple of classical times, being nearly twice the size of the Parthenon. It was considered as one of the seven wonders of the world. In it were collected the greatest sculptures and paintings of the ancients.

The visitor to Ephesus is disappointed when he sees that site of this temple. It is simply a depression in an olive grove with a few boulders scattered over it. The temple was completely destroyed by fire by a madman called Herostrate. This outrage was actuated by his mania to be remembered in perpetuity. The British and Istanbul museums guard a few treasures excavated from the site. Some of the columns of Santa Sofia are said to have come originally from the temple of Diana.

In the classical city may be seen a very large amphitheatre, stadium, gymnasia and libraries in excellent state of preservation. There is also an immense agora surrounded by colonnaded walks. Its centre was occupied by a lake.

St. Paul and St. John both preached to the Ephesaans. The province of Asia Minor was entrusted to St. John, who resided in its capital—Ephesus. He wrote his gospel and died in the city. Over his tomb was raised a basilica which has been excellently excavated and restored.

Seven Sleepers

Nearby is the legendary seven sleepers cemetery. Seven youths who were persecuted during the reign of Diocletian fled to a cave for refuge and there fell asleep. They are reputed to have awoken only after two centuries had elapsed, and to have walked into Ephesus. The city was quite unfamiliar to them and to their joy they discovered that it had become a Christian city. They were finally buried in the cave where they had slumbered so long.

Besides its archaeological treasures, Ephesus is gaining great fame for possessing a tiny isolated house named the Panaya Kapulu.

IT IS STILL DEBATED WHETHER THE BLESSED VIRGIN MARY SPENT HER LAST YEARS ON EARTH IN JERUSALEM OR IN EPHESUS, BUT THE EPHESIAN THEORY IS GAINING STRENGTH. ITS EXPONENTS CLAIM THAT, WHEN ST. JOHN CAME TO EPHESUS, HE WAS ACCOMPANIED BY THE MOTHER OF GOD, WHO WAS ENTRUSTED INTO HIS CARE BY A COMMAND FROM THE CROSS.

The house lies at about two hours walk from Selchuk. It is situated facing the sea at the head of a well-wooded valley. The island of Samos is clearly visible from it. Here, it is contended, the Mother of God resided.

It has been purchased by a French order of nuns who have restored most simply and tastefully the crumbling two-room dwelling. It nestles amid terraced olive groves, and below it is a spring which sends water down in a river into the sea. Though it is a place of frequent pilgrimages, the tranquillity of its position has been left undisturbed. I have seen Moslems pray in the Panaya Kapulu oratory with Christians, for they honour its alleged occupant as the mother of one of their great prophets.

The Road Back

I arrived back in Istanbul in mid October, several weeks behind my schedule. I had learned that to hitch-hike across the Balkans was feasible, but I had now run out of my most valuable hitch-hiking asset—time. To take the Simplon Orient express seemed to be the only way of reaching Dublin before Christmas. I felt reluctant to adopt this course, as I had not once travelled by train through the previous four months. I earned enough money by writing a series of articles in an Istanbul daily to buy a third class ticket to Trieste.

The Simplon Orient express really becomes an express only after it emerges from Yugo-Slavia. Until then it is simply a carriage or two connected on to the end of several local trains running on a single track. In past years the interest of the journey has been reduced as it no longer passes through Bulgaria. It is diverted instead via Salonica.

The journey took six hours short of three days. Often in the bustling changing of trains, I was assailed by doubts, even greater than when I was hitch-hiking, of whether I would ever reach my destination.

MY LITTLE PAPER TICKET WAS CHECKED TWENTY-SEVEN TIMES DURING THE JOURNEY.

Homewards

On arrival in Trieste on a Saturday afternoon, I started to hitch-hike northwards. Waiting in the cold twilight air at the Italian Zone A frontier, I felt very pessimistic about my future progress. My only aim now was to reach Ireland as fast as possible. I felt confident that, after months of unbroken good luck, I would experience a period of equally bad fortune.

A car with only the driver stopped at the barrier. I noticed it carried an international registration plate marked "B". I would not allow myself to think of the tremendous possibilities. To my delight the driver said he would like me to keep him company during his long trip. He was going directly to Brussels! I arrived in Ireland from Trieste at a speed more in keeping with that of a private motorist than that of a hitch-hiker.

I should like to pay tribute to the innumerable people without whose kindness I could not have realised this memorable 12,000-mile tour.

81608602R00040